HOUSEPLANTS

The Gardener's Collection

Better Homes and Gardens® Books

Des Moines

MEREDITH® BOOKS
President, Book Group: Joseph J. Ward
Vice President and Editorial Director: Elizabeth P. Rice
Art Director: Ernest Shelton

HOUSEPLANTS
Senior Editor: Marsha Jahns
Editor: Patricia Pollock
Art Director: Michael Burns
Copy Editors: Durrae Johanek, Kay Sanders, David Walsh
Assistant Editor: Jennifer Weir
Administrative Assistant: Carla Horner
Special thanks: John Whitman

MEREDITH CORPORATION CORPORATE OFFICERS:
Chairman of the Executive Committee: E. T. Meredith III
Chairman of the Board, President
and Chief Executive Officer: Jack D. Rehm
Group Presidents:
    Joseph J. Ward, Books
    William T. Kerr, Magazines
    Philip A. Jones, Broadcasting
    Allen L. Sabbag, Real Estate
Vice Presidents:
    Leo R. Armatis, Corporate Relations
    Thomas G. Fisher, General Counsel and Secretary
    Larry D. Hartsook, Finance
    Michael A. Sell, Treasurer
    Kathleen J. Zehr, Controller and Assistant Secretary

*All of us at Meredith® Books are dedicated to providing you
with the information and ideas you need to garden
successfully. We guarantee your satisfaction with this book for
as long as you own it. If you have any questions, comments,
or suggestions, please write to us at:*

MEREDITH® BOOKS, Garden Books
Editorial Department, RW 240
1716 Locust St.
Des Moines, IA 50309-3023

Walk into any room that you really like and look around. Chances are, growing green plants—foliage or flowering—are part of the setting. They add something indefinable, something special. This book will help you pick the plants best suited for your home and tell you how to care for them, too.

Contents

PROPAGATING HOUSEPLANTS 32

DIRECTORY OF HOUSEPLANTS 40

TROUBLESHOOTING GUIDE 62

INDEX 64

Choosing Houseplants

Living, growing indoor plants add color, beauty, and a sense of life to our homes. Foliage houseplants, especially, offer diversity in size, form, leaf shape, and texture. Flowering plants boost our spirits with delicate, elegant blooms. Browse through this informative chapter for tips on selecting those best suited to you.

Abundant Variety

Select plants that match your decorating needs and the growing conditions in your home.

Foliage plants are the backbone of most household plant collections. In full form year-round, they provide varied shades of green, a rich variety of textures, and shapes from massive to minute. Plants can be found to match the conditions in most any spot, from a bright window to a dim bathroom.

Flowering plants add not only bright splashes of color but also exquisite scents. Some are difficult to raise indoors or are seasonal gift plants. Others are less temperamental and bloom year after year. The secret is to match the plants'

needs for light and humidity with your time and home's conditions.

Though the most well-known plants fall into the categories described below, there are many others to inspire individuality.

Ferns are a class of foliage plant with 6,000 species. These thrive in indirect light and look delicate but are deceptively sturdy.

Palms also are dramatic foliage plants. They put out new growth in the winter and are well suited to summering outdoors.

Bromeliads are easy to grow and almost foolproof, usually blessed with exotic stiff leaves and bright, bold, unusual flowers.

Succulents are a huge family of plants with great diversity, unique forms, and sculpted shapes that result from stored water.

African violets now come in tiny miniature forms.

Gardener's Tip

Very small individual plants tend to dry out quickly in small pots. Try combining several miniatures in a basket to increase moisture.

Shopping Tips

Garden centers and florist shops are the best places to look for houseplants. Choose reputable stores where plants receive proper care. Some varieties may be available only by mail or from a plant society. Be sure the company has a money-back guarantee. Rare and unusual plants can be started from seeds ordered through mail-order companies.

Buyer's Checklist

■ Examine plants before buying. Foliage plants should be lush and full, have good color and firm leaves and stem, and be free of wilted or distorted leaves.

Gardener's Tip

Look for plants showing new growth. The foliage should be natural, not covered with a film of polish or wax.

■ Unless there's a good reason to buy flowers in full bloom, choose plants loaded with buds instead. This way, you can enjoy the whole show, not just the final act.

■ Look for insects and disease where branches join the stem. Plants displayed outdoors during warmer months attract insects.

■ Check the soil with your fingers. It shouldn't be too loose or too compact. Repot any with poor soil.

■ Package plants properly for the ride home. Warm the car in winter and make sure plants are wrapped. In summer, buy plants with well-moistened soil.

■ Wind may damage large plants transported in the open; wrap in heavy plastic or cloth.

■ Once home, label the new plant with date of purchase, source, plant type, and variety.

Several firecracker flowers are in this basket. They rarely grow more than 12 inches tall and do well in a south or west window.

Plants for Different Light Conditions

HIGH LIGHT

Plants in this list need high light at certain stages of development for best growth or flowering. Many also thrive in medium light. High light in winter is comparable to medium light the rest of the year.

Aloe
Amaryllis
Asparagus fern
Banana plant
Christmas cactus
Coleus
Croton
Cymbidium
Dragon tree
Fuchsia
Gardenia
Geranium
German ivy
Gloxinia
Grape ivy
Hibiscus
Hydrangea
Jade plant
Kalanchoe
Lady's-slipper
Podocarpus
Poinsettia
Snake plant
Swedish ivy
Umbrella plant
Wandering Jew
Wax begonia
Wax plant
Yucca
Zebra plant

MEDIUM LIGHT

Keep in mind that although some plants tolerate low light, it often retards bloom in flowering plants. It can affect color, shape, size, and number of leaves in foliage plants.

Achimenes
African violet
Arrowhead vine
Avocado
Azalea
Baby's-tears
Bird's-nest fern
Boston fern
Brake fern
Caladium
Camellia
Cast-iron plant
Chinese evergreen
Corn plant

Creeping Charlie
Cyclamen
Dieffenbachia
English ivy
False aralia
Fiddleleaf fig
Holly fern
Impatiens
Maidenhair fern
Ming aralia
Moth orchid
Nerve plant
Norfolk Island pine
Peperomia
Philodendron
Pleomele
Pocketbook flower
Prayer plant
Rex begonia
Rubber tree
Schefflera
Screw pine
Spathiphyllum
Spider plant
Staghorn fern
Swiss-cheese plant
Ti plant
Tuberous begonia
Weeping fig

The screw pine needs medium light; avoid full sun.

Plants for Special Purposes

Gift Houseplants
African violet
Amaryllis
Azalea
Chrysanthemum
Cyclamen
Cymbidium
Easter lily
Gloxinia
Poinsettia

Scented Houseplants
Easter lily
Gardenia
Geranium (some)
Hyacinth
Lemon tree
Paper-white narcissus

Unusual Houseplants
Banana plant
Bird-of-paradise
Ornamental pepper
Staghorn fern

Fun for Kids
Avocado (from pit)
Banana plant (with
  patience)
Spider plant
Sweet potato
Ti plant
Venus's-flytrap

Dangerous for Kids
Azalea
Caladium
Dieffenbachia
English ivy
Geranium (some)
Hyacinth
Hydrangea
Jerusalem cherry
Philodendron
Poinsettia

Climbing Plants
Arrowhead vine
English ivy
German ivy
Grape ivy
Philodendron
Sweet potato

Hanging Plants
African violet (some)
Arrowhead vine
Baby's-tears
Creeping Charlie
English ivy
Fuchsia
German ivy
Grape ivy
Philodendron
Spider plant
Staghorn fern
Swedish ivy
Sweet potato
Wandering Jew

Large or Treelike
Avocado
Banana plant
Camellia
Corn plant
Croton
Dieffenbachia
Dragon tree
False aralia
Fiddleleaf fig
Gardenia
Hibiscus

Hydrangea
Jade plant
Norfolk Island pine
Palm
Pleomele
Rubber plant
Schefflera
Screw pine
Snake plant
Swiss-cheese plant
Ti plant
Umbrella plant
Weeping fig

Cyclamen—showy gift plants clustered here in a basket—put on a dazzling display for months.

Small or Tabletop
African violet
Baby's-tears
Cast-iron plant
Coleus
Creeping Charlie
Lady's-slipper
Peperomia
Venus's-flytrap
Wax begonia

Colorful Foliage
Caladium
Coleus
Croton

Nerve plant
Prayer plant
Rex begonia

Easy-Care Plants
African violet
Aloe
Arrowhead vine
Asparagus fern
Baby's-tears
Cast-iron plant
Chinese evergreen
Coleus
Creeping Charlie
Dieffenbachia
English ivy

German ivy
Grape ivy
Jade plant
Peperomia
Philodendron
Rubber plant
Schefflera
Snake plant
Spider plant
Swedish ivy
Swiss-cheese plant
Ti plant
Wandering Jew

Tabletop Gardens

A refreshing change of pace from the one-plant–one-pot look is a lively grouping of plants in one large container.

Indoor Forest It's easy to re-create the aura of a forest in springtime. Line a basket with a 2-inch-thick layer of moistened sphagnum moss. Fill the basket with a potting mix of equal parts peat moss, soil, and perlite. Use a small trowel or tablespoon to plant ferns. For color, add pots of miniature African violets or primulas, making sure you sink the pots in the soil.

Use lukewarm water to keep the soil slightly moist, not soggy, when it begins to dry. Set in bright, indirect light, not direct sun. Mist the ferns daily and keep them away from drafts and heat sources. Feed blooming plants twice a month with a dilute liquid fertilizer.

Forcing Bulbs Tulips and daffodils can bloom on your windowsill even while winter rages outdoors when you create artificial, shorter seasons. Here are some tips.

■ Use a pot twice as tall as bulbs.

■ Put in as many bulbs as you can without letting them touch, flat side of tulips out. Set bulb tips even with pot rim. Cover with soil.

■ Water, then label pots. Move pots to cold storage.

■ Allow 15 weeks from potting to bloom. Most require 12 weeks of cold for rooting, plus 3 weeks at room temperature to flower. (Tulips need 15 weeks for rooting; narcissus, only three.)

■ Simulate winter cold and darkness in a refrigerator, cool basement, or garage. Temperatures should be 35–50 degrees Fahrenheit and never below freezing. Keep soil moist.

Gardener's Tip

In a big hurry? Buy ready-to-bloom plants and transplant them into one large container.

■ When stems are an inch or two high and roots are growing through the drainage holes, move to a cool room in your house, away from direct sunlight. When shoots are about 4 inches tall, set pots in a warm, bright area to stimulate blooming. Keep soil moist.

A single pot can display a colorful array of bulbs.

Caring for Houseplants

*K*eeping your plants healthy and happy is a simple matter of knowing how much light, water, and fertilizer they need. Ask questions when you purchase or receive a new plant. Try to provide your plants with growing conditions as nearly perfect as you can— then just sit back and enjoy them.

Container and Soil Savvy

Most houseplants are sold in standard plastic pots with less-than-ideal soil. Give some thought to both before leaving the plant in that condition.

Containers Clay pots have been popular with gardeners for years and work well because they let air in and moisture out. They come in many sizes, including hand-molded shapes. Always soak new clay pots in water overnight before using. Scrub old pots between plantings, or, if disease has been a problem, soak in a bleach solution (1 part bleach to 9 parts water). Rinse.

■ Glazed or plastic pots stay clean more easily than clay pots. They also are cheaper, lighter, and come in more colors. Plants will need fewer waterings, but because these pots let in less air, watering and feeding must be more exact.

■ All containers should have drainage holes in the bottom. If you want to use decorative items like old crocks, put pots with drainage holes inside the crocks. Each pot needs a plastic or clay saucer to collect the excess water.

■ You also can use plastic buckets, milk cartons, window boxes, and such. Use a drill, hot ice pick, or knife to cut a drain hole, if needed.

■ Pots come in a variety of sizes; the width of the opening at the top determines its size.

Soil You can buy potting soil or mix your own. For an all-purpose formula, use one part sand (or perlite or vermiculite), one part peat moss, and two parts loamy garden soil. Sterilize any of the ingredients that could contain weed seeds, insects, or diseases by baking them in a 200° oven for 45 minutes. Purchased potting soils already are sterilized.

Gardener's Tip

A new, unconditioned clay pot tends to draw water out of the soil, robbing the plant. To avoid this, completely immerse the pot in a pail of water. Let stand till all bubbling and hissing stop.

For succulents or African violets, add more sand or peat moss or buy special mixes. Orchids need a special soilless mixture such as fern bark or osmunda fiber.

Whatever you use, be sure the soil is neither powdery dry nor soggy. Store it in a closed plastic bag or container.

Buy premixed potting soil or mix your own. Clockwise from right: vermiculite, sand, black loam, perlite, and peat moss.

Repotting and Potting Up

If a plant is thriving, assume it is happy in its pot. Some plants, though, may need repotting right after you buy them, especially if young and actively growing. Garden-center plants often are root-bound, and the soil used may not be the best.

Taking a plant out of a pot and putting it back in the same-size pot is called repotting. Putting it in a larger pot is called potting up. The technique is similar.

Repotting Do this to improve the soil when the plant is new, or to switch to a more decorative—or different type of—pot. For plants that go dormant, repot at the end of the dormant period, just before the plant's active growing season.

To check the roots, gently knock the plant out of the pot. Healthy white roots should be numerous around the outside of the root ball, but not crowded into a solid mass or winding round and round in a tangle. Pot up if the roots have nowhere left to grow.

Potting Up Young seedlings and cuttings need potting up frequently for growth to continue unchecked. If you notice that growth slows in an older plant or if it wilts too soon after watering, lower leaves turn yellow, or new leaves stay small, it's time to look at the root ball. If you receive a gift planter with several plants crowded together, pot them up soon so they will have room to spread naturally.

Gardener's Tip

The day before repotting or potting up, moisten the soil. This makes it easier to get the plant out and helps shield the plant from the trauma of the change. Soil should be firmly moist, not dry or soggy.

How to Pot Up:

■ Select the new pot, usually one size larger (½ to 1 inch) than the present pot. Put a crockery shard over the bottom hole to keep the soil in the pot. Large pots should have a layer of shards.

■ To loosen the plant, put one hand over the soil and around the stem. Turn the pot over and rap it firmly against a hard surface. The soil and roots usually come out in a compact unit. If they don't, run a knife between the soil and pot to loosen.

■ Keep the root ball as intact as possible, unless the roots have become a snarl. If they're snarled, loosen some of them around the edges and bottom; trim broken or soft roots.

■ Place the plant in the center of the pot with the base of the stem about ½ to 1 inch below the pot rim. Fill with soil around the root ball, burying the plant to the same level. Tap pot; add soil as needed.

■ Water plant immediately. Keep in indirect light until it shows new growth. Keep moist, never soggy.

When potting up, go up one size. If a plant was in a 4-inch pot, use a 5-inch (not 6-inch) pot.

Press added soil firmly around the plant in the new pot. Tap the pot to even the soil and eliminate air pockets. Add more soil.

Lighting Requirements

Proper light is critical for success with houseplants. Check the lists on pages 12 and 13 to find out what kind of light a plant needs before you purchase it. If it needs more than you have available, pass it up until you can provide it with the necessary light through grow-lights or additional windows.

The Directory of Houseplants (pages 40–61) also indicates the ideal lighting conditions.

There are a few general rules, but all have exceptions. For the most part, flowering plants need more light than foliage plants (yet croton, a foliage plant, needs lots of light to keep its vibrant leaf color). Most plants with thick, fleshy leaves need little light (yet cacti and succulents thrive in bright light).

Some plants flower according to how long light is present each day, rather than how intense it is. Christmas cactus, chrysanthemum, kalanchoe, and poinsettia are examples of plants that need short days (long nights) to flower properly.

High light is found in a greenhouse or by a window with a southern or southwestern exposure. This is intense light, as strong as can be found indoors. It also is referred to as full sun.

Medium light refers to direct exposure from an east or west window. Also receiving medium light (or what's called bright indirect) are spots near a filtered southern or southwestern exposure (or some distance from a similar exposure that's unfiltered).

Low light is found near north windows. The light several feet from an east or west window or far from a southern or southwestern exposure (in both cases, often called indirect light) also qualifies as low light. Low light is common in corners and bathrooms; it is not total darkness.

Artificial Light Many houseplants thrive in artificial light. The most inexpensive artificial source is a fluorescent tube.

Too much intense sun (right) caused this peperomia's leaves to be sickly, lifeless, and colorless. Remove the lackluster leaves and move the plant away from direct sun.

Carefully position plants under the light source (as close as 6 inches, never more than 15 inches away). Keep light on for as many as 16 hours a day, depending on your plant. To increase light intensity, use more tubes, add reflectors, or leave lights on longer. Rotate plants regularly.

Flowering plants fail to bud or bloom in poor artificial light. Foliage plants needing more light get tall and spindly; exposed to too much light they're ghostly or faded.

Too little light caused these mature schefflera leaves (above) to turn yellow. New leaves that grow small and spindly also are a sign of low light.

Water and Temperature Tips

Water Although the need for water is obvious, the solution is all too subtle. You can kill your plants with either neglect or kindness.

Always use tepid water. Cold water can slow growth or injure roots. Softened water also is hard on plants. If your water is high in chlorine, let it stand a day uncovered before using it.

The plant's condition often tells you when to water. Use your finger to test the soil surface for moisture. Small pots may need water every day or two. Large ones may go a week between waterings. Check often; experience soon will tell you what to do.

The amount of water, fortunately, is easier to figure than the frequency. Add water until it drains through the hole in the bottom of the pot and shows in the saucer. This ensures that the entire root area receives a thorough soaking. The roots need air, too, so be sure to empty the saucer 20 minutes after watering.

Temperature Just as plants vary in their need for moisture, they also vary in their temperature requirements. Some plants like it cool; others, tropical.

Most houseplants do well in average house temperatures. To encourage best growth, turn the thermostat down at night. Plants like a 10-degree temperature drop after dark, similar to what they experience in nature.

To grow plants that like cool conditions, keep the thermostat between 60 and 70 degrees in the day, lower at night. For plants that like high temperatures, set the thermostat in the 80s during the day and lower at night.

Prevent cold drafts or blasts of hot air near plants; keep plants away from cold windows and radiators in winter.

Summering Plants Most indoor plants take well to a move outdoors for the summer. Do this after all danger of frost has passed. Move plants first into shade, then into indirect light, and finally, if they are

full-sun plants, into bright light. This process, known as hardening off, takes about 14 days.

Place houseplants outside in locations that match their indoor light preferences. Water frequently; mist to increase humidity, kill insects, and cleanse. At season's end, spray plants with insecticide before bringing them indoors. Avoid frost damage; better to bring them in too early than too late.

Using a long-spout watering can, pour until water runs out the drainage hole. Let the plant drain, then dump the excess water.

Humidity and Feeding Hints

Humidity Most plants need more humidity than usually is found in a home, especially when the furnace or air conditioner is running. You can ease this problem with a whole-house humidifier, but there are other ways, too.

Frequent misting of the plants will help. So will setting them on trays of pebbles kept wet (but don't let the pots themselves stand in water). Just grouping plants together helps, too.

During weather extremes, when the furnace or air conditioner runs nonstop, you might run a cool vaporizer or put a problem plant in a plastic bag. Make use of places in your home with the highest humidity: the laundry, bathroom, and over the kitchen sink.

Feeding Plants Feeding instructions may seem more confusing than those for watering, but they also are less critical. Buy a good, balanced houseplant fertilizer for most indoor plants, a specialized one if you have many African violets, bromeliads, or orchids.

Read the label. The three numbers (such as 10-20-10) refer to the levels of nitrogen, phosphorus, and potassium. Nitrogen gives the plant lush foliage. Phosphorus keeps roots and stems strong and healthy. Potassium encourages blooms.

Organic fertilizers are blood meal, bonemeal, cow manure, fish emulsion, and kelp products. Chemical fertilizers are sold under a variety of product names, and chemical analysis varies by brand. Read labels.

Water the day before feeding. Fertilizers—most for houseplants come in solution form—can burn if the soil is dry. Getting the solution on the leaves will give them a good foliar feeding; avoid fertilizing the flowers, however, or spotting could result. Follow directions or give less. Never give more.

Plants need little feeding in the winter when they are almost dormant, more in the spring and summer when they are growing more actively.

For plants that have grown large, such as the rubber plant taking over the bedroom or the philodendron covering a window, give the minimum amount of food to purposely keep growth slow.

Do not feed seedlings until they have their first true leaves, and then use a diluted dose. Hold off feeding new or repotted plants for several weeks until they've had time to adjust to their new home. And remember, feeding is seldom the cure for a sick plant.

Keep plants healthy for up to three weeks while you're away by watering them, then covering them with makeshift plastic tents. Use bamboo stakes or bent clothes hangers to support the plastic above the plant leaves.

Houseplant Beauty Cues

Simple little tricks can make a big difference in the appearance of the healthiest plants and perk up the ones with minor ailments.

■ Give your plants a quarter to half turn each week. This will give them nice rounded shapes. Turning also lets you see the other side of your plants and the shades and shapes of leaves and flowers.

■ Take pot in hand and remove the dead leaves that sneak under the lushest foliage. Give the pot a firm tap on a hard surface to settle the roots. Soak the pot in the sink for a half hour to dissolve the salts in the soil (soaking also will moisten the pores of a clay pot).

■ To give shape to plants like philodendron and ivy, wind the long, trailing branches up over the pot in a pleasing pattern, then pin them to the soil at several points with hairpins, bent pipe cleaners, or bent paper clips. Do this every few months. The branches probably will root at these points, giving you a lusher-looking plant.

■ Some plants need to be trimmed into shape. Remember that taking off end growth encourages side branches just below the cut.

■ Help your plants breathe by cleaning their leaves. You can clean many plants quickly under the shower if you have unsoftened water. Wrap plastic bags around the bases to keep the soil in the pots, then wash with lukewarm water at low to medium force. Let the plants drip-dry. If chemical residue in the water leaves white spots, wipe the spots away with a clean, soft cloth.

■ If the weather is warm, set plants outdoors in the rain. Shower large plants with a spray bottle.

■ You can give your plants that florist shine with special sprays or liquids, or with a cloth dipped in milk. But try not to get any of these solutions on the leaf undersides. You might clog the stomata, the leaves' breathing organs.

■ To clean the dust from large, smooth-leaved plants, hold one hand under a leaf and wipe gently with a rag in the other.

■ Use a dry cotton swab, pipe cleaner, or watercolor brush to softly clean hairy-leaved plants, such as African violet and gloxinia.

■ Watch closely for insects, and wash them away with soapy water. Vigilance is the best cure for insect problems. If you use sprays, put the plants in plastic bags to concentrate the effect. Higher humidity also eases plant stress. Systemic insecticides go into the soil and up through the roots to the entire plant to kill insects.

(See the Troubleshooting Guide, pages 62–63, for more help.)

Wash plants often in lukewarm water (above) to rid of dust and insects. Place in sink; let drip-dry.

Prune an indoor tree (right) to give it a pleasing and sturdy shape. Always cut away any dead or broken branches.

Propagating Plants

The easiest, most inexpensive way to add plants to your collection is to propagate those you already have. Multiplying them yourself will give you the added pleasure of watching baby plants grow up. Depending on the plant, methods include seeds, root divisions, runners and offsets, cuttings (leaf, stem, or root), and air layering.

Seeds and Root Division

Seeds are a satisfying way to start many houseplants, including asparagus fern, bromeliads, cacti, coleus, gloxinia, impatiens, and kalanchoe.

Begin with a fine, sterile medium such as potting soil, sand, vermiculite, perlite, or peat moss; cover with ¼ inch of milled sphagnum moss. Sprinkle seeds across the moss surface or into shallow rows.

Mist with water. Cover the tray with glass or plastic; place on a heating pad (the top of the refrigerator also works). Follow lighting instructions on the seed packet. Mist whenever the medium starts to dry.

When seedlings appear, remove the cover and begin watering the surface whenever the soil starts to dry out. Nighttime dampness encourages mold and fungus, so water early in the morning. Turn the pan or pot periodically—or set under grow-lights—to keep plants growing straight, instead of leaning toward the window.

Thin out the seedlings if you plan to keep the plants in the same pot. If not, transplant when the first true pair of leaves appears (it's the second set of leaves) and plant them in their own small pots. Water again; move plants progressively to brighter light. Fertilize mildly—half the suggested amount diluted in water—every two weeks.

Root division is actually the splitting or cutting up of one plant into two or more parts. Almost any plant that grows from several stems in one pot can be divided. This includes peperomias, most ferns, cast-iron plant, creeping Charlie, and prayer plant. Early spring is usually the best time.

To divide a plant, gently knock it out of its container. Remove the root ball and shake off as much soil as you can. Then gently break the root ball apart to see how the roots are growing to determine the way to divide it.

For example, spider plants actually put out new stems and plants next to the original plant,

similar to a sucker or offset. Separate these and repot. The roots of the sprengeri asparagus fern simply build on each other to make one large root ball; cut these apart. Don't be afraid to use a knife; it's better to cleanly sever the roots than to tear them into pieces. Asparagus ferns often have so many roots you must discard some.

Put the divisions into smaller pots. Water thoroughly, and set in indirect light for a week or two while the plant adjusts.

Dividing roots is one way to enlarge your houseplant collection.

Bulbs also are propagated by root division. The amaryllis and oxalis form offsets that can be cut from the parent plant and potted individually. Propagate before new growth starts in the spring. The tuberous begonia and caladium can be propagated by dividing their tubers into two or more parts and potting them separately. Spring is the best time for dividing.

Runners, Tip Cuts, and Stem Cuts

Runners—the small plantlets that form on aerial shoots (such as on spider plants, piggyback plants)—are easy to propagate. Fill a pot with peat-based rooting medium, and pin the plantlet into the medium with a hairpin or bent paper clip, keeping the plantlet moist until it takes root. Then, sever the stem to the parent plant. Rooting this way takes four to five weeks.

Tip Cuttings Propagating houseplants from cuttings is probably the most common method. Do this in the spring. Almost any plant with trailing stems can be multiplied from tip cuttings. Try coleus, wandering Jew, Swedish ivy, and philodendron.

Select a mature, healthy tip of the main stem or side branch; use a sharp knife or blade to cut just below a leaf node (the place where a leaf grows from the stem). The cutting should be several inches long and have four to six healthy leaves. Remove leaves from the bottom of the piece so they won't be buried in the rooting medium; dip the cuttings in a rooting hormone, if you wish.

Many cuttings will root in plain water, but roots grown in water tend to be brittle and fragile; they often break off as you pot the plant. You'll have better luck using a soilless medium, such as perlite, vermiculite, sand, peat moss, or any mixture of these. Equal portions of perlite and peat moss make a good combination.

If you're rooting only two or three cuttings, a small clay pot works well. If you're rooting more, use a clear plastic shoe box or other larger flat, covered container.

Moisten the rooting mixture and poke holes in it with a knife or pencil. Slip the cuttings in and gently firm soil around the stems.

Mist lightly and cover with the lid or encase in a plastic bag and close tightly. Place under fluorescent lights or in indirect light. In several weeks, check to see whether the cuttings have rooted by giving each a gentle tug. If the cutting resists, it should be sufficiently rooted to pot. (There should be an inch or two of roots.) If the cutting isn't sufficiently rooted, return it to the medium.

When rooting runners, pin the plantlet to the medium with a hairpin or bent paper clip

Stem Cuttings New plants can be produced from sections of stem, especially dieffenbachia and dracaena. Stem cuttings should be 4 to 6 inches long and include one or more nodes. Place each stem section in a moist rooting medium, just covering the nodes with soil. Keep moist. In a few weeks, you'll see new growth. Pot when roots are strong.

Root cuttings (2-inch sections of the plant's root) also can be potted in moist rooting medium.

Cuttings from plants with multiple stems are successfully rooted when the tip is 4 to 6 inches long and includes a leaf node.

Leaf Cuttings and Air Layering

Leaf Cuttings Follow the same procedure for rooting leaf cuttings as described for stem cuttings (a leaf stalk rather than the central stem is used). Take leaf cuttings of such plants as peperomia, hoya, begonia, African violet, and many of the succulents.

Simply cut off a mature, healthy leaf at the stem base with a sharp knife and insert it in a moist rooting medium. In several weeks, tiny leaves will push their way up through the soil. When leaves and stems are strong and healthy, sever plantlets from the parent leaf and pot up individually.

If you're rooting only one leaf, especially the woody-stemmed ones, you can put it in a small plastic bag filled with rooting medium. When the leaf has developed strong roots, pot it and watch for new leaves to emerge. When they do, remove and discard the old leaf.

Many leaf cuttings also will root in water. Simply cover a jar or cup of water with aluminum foil, poke holes in it, and insert one or more leaf cuttings.

To root cuttings of snake plant, cut a mature, healthy leaf into 3-inch segments; place upright in a growing medium so half of each section is buried (sections will not root if upside down). In a couple of months, new shoots will form at the side. Remove when roots are sufficiently strong.

Air layering is more a way to revitalize plants than to propagate them. Through air layering, top-heavy, woody-stemmed plants are induced to grow new roots higher up on the stem.

You can air layer schefflera, dieffenbachia, ficus, and dracena species that have lost their bottom leaves. Use a sharp knife to make a cut approximately one-third of the way down the stem. Make an upward slit, cut a notch out of the stem, or just scrape away enough of the bark to expose the plant tissue. Don't cut more than halfway through the stem. If you simply slit the stem, hold the cut open with a toothpick or matchstick.

Next, wrap a baseball-size clump of sphagnum moss around the stem where you've made the cut; wrap with plastic, and secure with wire twists or string.

Periodically check the moss for moisture. If it has dried out, mist lightly and rewrap the plastic. In several weeks (or months, depending on the plant), you'll see roots forming. When they fill the plastic wrap, cut the stem off below the new roots; then plant, moss and all.

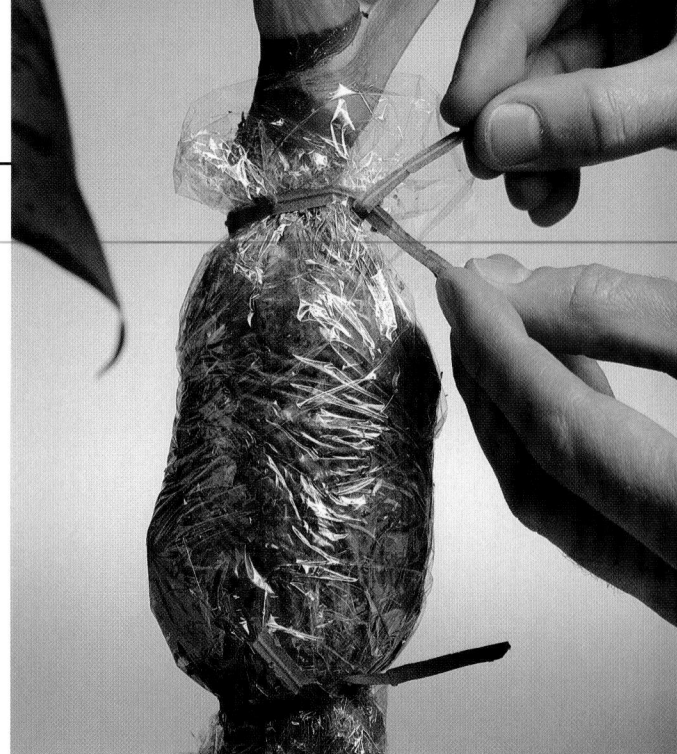

Remember you'll be opening the plastic to mist the moss inside.

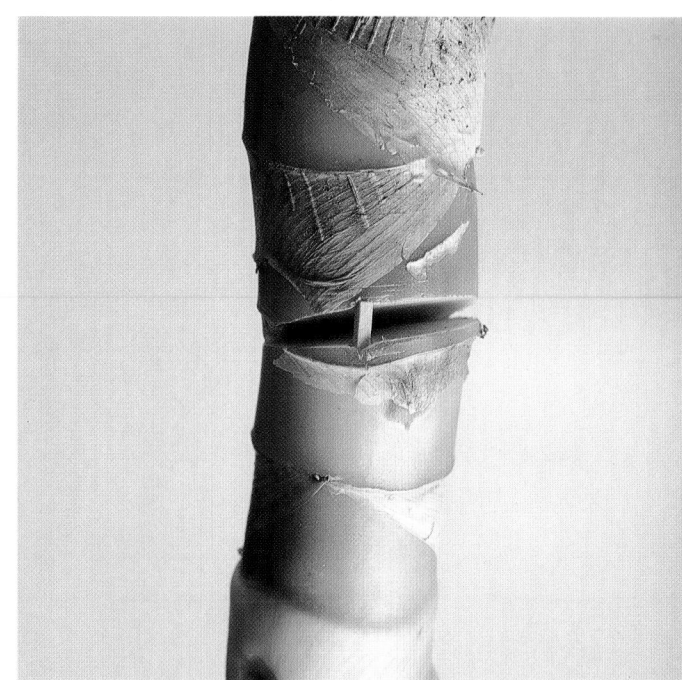

Air layering's critical cut is held open with a wooden pick or matchstick..

Directory of Houseplants

*A*lmost everyone can have green-thumb success with indoor plants when this plant directory is at hand. Both foliage and flowering houseplants are described in considerable detail. You'll also find guidelines on lighting, watering, temperature, and propagation.

Foliage Plants

ALOE
(Burn plant, first aid plant, medicinal aloe, unguentine cactus)
Aloe sp.

Foliage: Aloe is a succulent with thick, fleshy leaves that thrives in hot, dry conditions. Pluck a leaf, peel away the skin and spines, and use the fluid to treat burns, mosquito bites, diaper rash, and all sorts of minor skin irritations.

Light: Place in bright south windows for best results, although plant will tolerate moderate light. Outside in summer, plant in some shade or move into sun gradually.

Water: Allow to dry between waterings. Water less in winter.

Comments: Allow temperatures to climb to 80s during the day, 10 degrees less at night. Increase plants with offsets. It blooms if the light is bright enough long enough, but seldom indoors.

ARALIA, FALSE
(Threadleaf)
Dizygotheca elegantissima

Foliage: Grows slowly to 5 feet and has delicate, dark green to almost reddish brown leaves arranged like fingers in a fan shape.

Light: Bright indirect light. It will thrive for years with only artificial overhead light. Summer outdoors; stake to protect from wind.

Water: Water thoroughly; keep soil evenly moist.

Comments: Maintain temperatures in low 60s for best growth. Tolerates average temperatures. Use standard potting mix. Feed lightly every 2 weeks during active growth. Propagate by stem cuttings or root divisions.

ASPARAGUS FERN
(Lace fern)
Asparagus setaceus

Foliage: Graceful, lacy foliage often used in hanging baskets.

Light: Place in high light in fall and winter, southeastern exposure in spring and summer.

Water: Keep soil evenly moist. Mist daily to raise humidity.

Comments: Maintain average temperatures but never below 50 at night. Cut back regularly; grows rapidly. Feed monthly during active growth, less rest of the year. Propagate by division.

AVOCADO
(Alligator pear)
Persea americana

Foliage: Grows from the pit of the fruit. When plant gets 6 leaves, cut it back to 2. Also pinch branch tips as they form to keep plants from getting too tall and skinny. Treelike shape.

Light: Place in bright to indirect sun. Grows in full sun outdoors in subtropics.

Water: Let dry between waterings. Good drainage prevents root rot.

Comments: To start, select ripest fruit. Remove and clean pit; let stand in a warm spot overnight. Peel off skin; insert 3 toothpicks around the fattest part of the pit. Rest picks on the edge of a jar so water just covers the flat-bottom end of pit. Pot up when rooted. Seed splits as a tiny stem arises in 4 to 8 weeks, sooner at 85 degrees. Keep seed out of direct sun until growth starts.

BABY'S-TEARS
(Japanese moss, Irish moss)
Helxine soleiroli or Soleirolia soleiroli

Foliage: Slender, horizontal stems, crowded with tiny round leaves; won't grow far over the edge of a pot because they must have contact with the soil.

Light: Bright indirect light.

Water: Even moisture and high humidity.

Comments: Combine baby's-tears only with plants that are fairly thirsty. The leaves resent wetting, and the plant is sensitive to cooking or heating gas. Prefers soil high in peat. Propagate by division.

BOSTON FERN
Nephrolepis exaltata 'bostoniensis'

Foliage: Pale green leaves that can stretch 3 feet.

Light: Medium light of east window.

Water: Allow soil to become dry between thorough waterings. Mist. Raise humidity in warm weather.

Comments: Maintain up to 75-degree temperatures in daytime, no less than 50 at night. Use clay pots and porous soil. Pot up when severely root-bound. Avoid insecticides. Propagate by division in early spring or by runners (threads off side of plant).

CALADIUM
Caladium sp.

Foliage: Intricately marked leaves of white, pink, red, green, silver, and combinations of each. Remove insignificant blooms.

Light: Indoors, place in bright indirect light; outdoors, in shade. Hot sun can scorch leaves.

Water: Water when soil surface is dry. When in full leaf, caladiums can drink a lot. Provide good drainage. They like heat and humidity.

Comments: Start bulbs indoors in April in trays of vermiculite with bottom heat. Repot as they grow. Put outdoors only after the ground is warm and frost danger passes. Lift bulbs and bring inside for winter. Acid soil gives deepest colors. Propagate by bulb divisions.

CAST-IRON PLANT
(Barroom plant)
Aspidistra elatior

Foliage: Long, tapered, dark green or variegated leaves that arise on stems from a crown.

Light: Place near window out of direct sun for most luxuriant look. Will survive in dark corners.

Water: Let dry between soakings. Overwatering causes more problems than neglect.

Comments: Place in areas with temperatures from 45 to 85 degrees. The solid green varieties prefer rich

Cast-Iron Plant

soil. Variegated varieties will revert to all green in rich soil. Too much sun will yellow leaves. Trim off brown leaf tips. Propagate by cutting the root ball apart with a sharp knife.

CHINESE EVERGREEN
(Chinese waterplant, painted drop-tongue, spotted evergreen)
Aglaonema sp.

Foliage: Some varieties grow 15 to 24 inches tall; others grow 3 feet tall. Lance-shape leaves grow on thick stalks. Variegated type requires more light for best dappling.

Light: Place in north window or near center of room.

Water: Keep evenly moist. Plant can grow in water alone; add charcoal to keep water clear and soluble fertilizer occasionally after changing the water completely.

Comments: Needs temperatures in low 80s during the day and no less than the low 60s at night. Use all-purpose soil mixture. Tolerates heat and low humidity. Propagate by root division or stem cuttings.

COLEUS
(Painted nettle, flame nettle, painted leaves)
Coleus sp.

Foliage: Velvety leaves come in reds, greens, yellows, bronze, and chartreuse; leaf edges may be scalloped or ruffled.

Light: Provide bright or indirect light indoors, sun or shade outside. Good on the north or east side of building. Lack of light dulls colors.

Water: Keep evenly moist for lush growth. Leaves will wilt if thirsty; revive with water or evening dew.

Comments: Remove spikes of purple flowers; pinch for bushy growth. Use standard soil mix. Feed once a month during the growing season. Replace old plants with new cuttings once a year, or start from seeds for new colors. Plants will root in water.

CORN PLANT
Dracaena fragrans 'massangeana'

Foliage: Leaves resemble corn leaves, only thicker and darker green with stripes. Stalks will grow very tall, often woody and bare, with a cluster of leaves at the end.

Light: Place in east window or out of direct sun in south or west exposure. Leaf edges will develop brown spots in too much sun.

Water: Keep soil just moist to the touch. Lower leaves may drop off if plant gets too dry.

Comments: Aim for 60- to 75-degree temperatures. Strip lower leaves for accent. Use a loose, humus-rich soil mix with good drainage. Feed every 3 months year-round. Plant 3 in a tub with leaf tops at different heights for drama. Propagate from tip cuttings or pieces of stem with buds, or by air layering. New growth will sprout from stub.

CREEPING CHARLIE
Pilea nummulariifolia

Foliage: Light green leaves on reddish stems; grows well in hanging baskets. (Note: not the same as garden creeping Charlie.)

Light: Bright or indirect sun.

Water: Keep evenly moist.

Comments: Likes average temperatures, 65 to 75 degrees. Add extra peat moss for a rich potting soil. Feed lightly every 2 months; keep humidity high. Pinch leggy growing tips. Propagate by stem cuttings or division.

CROTON
(Garden croton, Joseph's coat, variegated laurel)
Codiaeum sp.

Foliage: Long, waxy leaves are spectacular, with bright colors, patterns, and blotches of yellow, pink, red, and bronze.

Light: Provide strong light at least 4 hours a day, or leaves will revert to green. Colors return if placed outdoors in summer, but harden the plant carefully both going out in summer and coming back in fall.

Water: Keep soil evenly moist. Mist daily to provide humidity.

Comments: Maintain average temperatures; avoid drafts, which cause leaf drop. Use rich potting mixture with good drainage. Feed every other month from early spring through midsummer. Multiply by stem cuttings, or air layer in spring or summer.

DIEFFENBACHIA
(Dumb cane, mother-in-law-plant, tuftroot)
Dieffenbachia sp.

Foliage: Called dumb cane because sap can cause swelling of the tongue and vocal cords and a loss of voice. Aoid putting your fingers near your mouth or eyes. This evergreen grows 6 feet or more in height with a thick trunk and large, patterned 1½-foot leaves that arch gracefully.

Light: Offer north, east, or west light with no more than 2 hours of daily sun. Plant tolerates a wide range of light, but full sun can yellow its foliage.

Water: Let the soil dry on the surface between waterings. Occasionally, immerse pot or move plant to a steamy bathroom.

Comments: This tropical native likes heat—temperatures into the 80s by day, no less than 60s at night. Feed monthly in spring and summer. Expect lower leaves to die. When the leggy stem becomes unsightly, air layer. Also will root in water. A new stem will sprout on the stub, so cut to desired height.

ENGLISH IVY
Hedera helix

Foliage: A hardy ground cover turned houseplant. Train plants on supports for special shapes. Several varieties offer a choice of leaf shapes, sizes, variegations, textures, and habit.

Light: Offer filtered light or a north window.

Water: Keep evenly moist, well drained, and a bit drier in winter.

Comments: Place in cool spots, 55 degrees at night. Shower or mist both sides of leaves weekly to combat mites. Roots in water.

FIDDLE-LEAF FIG
Ficus lyrata

Foliage: Shiny, leathery leaves in the shape of a violin.

Light: Place in bright, indirect sun. Full sun can burn this plant.

Water: Water well when soil surface dries. As plant grows, be sure water reaches bottom of pot but does not gather and sit.

Comments: High temperatures for best growth. Use all-purpose potting soil lightened with a little sand or perlite. Feed 3 or 4 times a year unless the plant is growing too fast. Keep the leaves dusted clean. Pinch if you want branching. Propagate with tip cuttings in water or rooting media, or air layer.

JADE PLANT
(Chinese rubber plant)
Crassula argentea

Foliage: A popular succulent with jade-colored, round, fleshy leaves. It easily grows 3 feet or taller.

Light: Place in direct sunlight.

Water: Watch overwatering. Let the soil dry between waterings—it can wait as long as 2 weeks.

Comments: Repot using any soil. Plants usually live for years, even when root-bound. Don't feed plants except lightly in summer, or they may grow too fast. Prune for a more treelike shape. Leaves or tip cuttings root easily. Let them lie exposed for a week to form a callus before inserting in sand or perlite.

Norfolk Island Pine

NORFOLK ISLAND PINE
(Star pine)
Araucaria heterophylla

Foliage: Soft, short needles appear on horizontal branches from the trunk at yearly intervals in tiers of 6. Like an indoor evergreen.

Light: Place in medium light but not direct sunlight indoors or out. If the light is too low, too much space will develop between tiers.

Water: Allow to dry between waterings. Plants tolerate generous watering if drainage is excellent.

Comments: Maintain cool temperatures at night for best growth. Decorate these easy plants as Christmas trees, but avoid heavy or hot bulbs. Repot every 2 or 3 years and top-dress every March. Feed no more than once a month during spring and summer. If needles turn brown, cut off affected branches flush with the trunk. Side cuttings will give a one-sided plant. If plant gets leggy, cut off entire top and root it.

PALMS—GENERAL

Foliage: Palms are dramatic plants that create a lush tropical atmosphere and are easy to grow.

Light: Provide bright light indoors, even a bit of full sun in winter. Outside, filtered shade is best.

Water: Offer even moisture. Palms are not desert plants. Moisture is important to prevent browning. A plant in a 9-inch pot requires 1½ quarts of water each week. Mist often to increase humidity.

Comments: Pots should be deep to give roots enough room. Top-dress yearly. Repot only if so root-bound that water won't soak through. Use a porous, lime-type soil with excellent drainage. Feed a slow-release houseplant food every 3 or 4 months. When plants are near the size you want, feed them just once in the spring. Feed potentially tall or spreading plants less frequently than naturally short ones. Summer outdoors; offer wind protection. Propagation by seeds or offsets is possible, but slow and impractical.

PEPEROMIA
(Many common names, most including the name peperomia)
Peperomia sp.

Foliage: Thick, semisucculent leaves may be smooth, shiny green, two-tone, corrugated, or deeply ridged, with red, pink, or green trailing or upright stems. Emerald-ripple peperomia has deeply ridged and quilted, dark green and brown, almost heart-shape leaves; ivy peperomia has a silver sheen on its round leaves; watermelon peperomia has stripes.

Light: Place in medium to bright light, but not direct sun. A bright north window is fine, but diffuse the sun in other windows.

Water: Allow to dry between waterings during winter. Keep evenly moist during active growth. Likes humidity.

Comments: Keep in warm room, 55 to 75 degrees. Use standard potting mix with added sand or perlite; repot infrequently. Feed no more than once a month during active growth, not at all in winter. Root tip cuttings of branching varieties, leaves of others. Plant just the base of the leaf in the medium. Crowns also can be divided on some peperomias.

PHILODENDRON
Philodendron sp.

Foliage: The most common variety has smooth, 3- to 4-inch heart-shape leaves. Selloum or saddle-leaf philodendron sends up leaves as large as 2 feet long.

Light: Place in bright indirect light; plants will live in low light.

Water: Provide ample water, keeping soil evenly moist. Many types appreciate a support wrapped with moist sphagnum moss. Water sphagnum, too.

Comments: Maintain temperatures in the 80s for best growth. Feed the plants every 3 or 4 months. Large

types send out long, ropelike aerial roots; stick into soil or clip off. Large types may form offsets around base that can be separated. Propagate by ground layering, stem cuttings, or seed.

PRAYER PLANT
(Maranta, rabbit's-foot, rabbit's-tracks, ten commandments)
Maranta sp.

Foliage: At night its leaves—oval with intricate texture and color— fold together.

Light: Place in medium to low light. Avoid all but cool morning sun. Lower light intensifies colors.

Water: Keep evenly moist and mist daily. Use tepid water. Leave slightly drier in winter.

Comments: Use high temperatures (80s) for best growth. Use a peat-rich soil mix and feed lightly only during the summer, not more than once a month. In January, trim back the older leaves, or cut stems back to the soil. Propagate by tip cuttings, air layering, division, or seed.

REX BEGONIA
Begonia x rex-cultorum

Foliage: Colored patterns, metallic markings on large leaves.

Light: Medium (bright indirect) light except in fall and winter, then less. Avoid full sun.

Water: Keep soil evenly moist; reduce in fall and winter. Do not mist, but raise humidity.

Comments: Plant rhizomes in shallow pot in peat-rich soil. When growing, feed every 14 days with dilute solution. In fall, let die back. Store in cool, dark spot until February, then water more and bring to light. Propagate by seed or leaf cuttings.

RUBBER PLANT
Ficus elastica

Foliage: A bold tree with large, rubbery leaves on straight stems. Many varieties.

Light: Expose to medium light. Tolerates low light.

Water: Allow soil to dry out between waterings. Mist often; raise humidity.

Comments: High temperatures make for best growth. Tolerates average temperatures. Pot up only when severely root-bound. Use porous soil. Pinch growing tip from young plant for multiple stem growth. Feed every 14 days with mild solution during active growth. Cut stem back to base if plant gets too large or leggy; stump regenerates. Root tip for another plant. Propagate by air layering, tip cuttings, or leaf-bud cuttings.

SCHEFFLERA
(Australian umbrella tree, Queensland umbrella tree, octopus tree)
Brassaia actinophylla

Foliage: The shiny horizontal leaves look like wheels, with 6- to 8-leaflet spokes about 1½ inches wide and 5 to 9 inches long.

Light: Give strong light but not direct sun. Turn plant often.

Water: Let soil surface dry between waterings. More tolerant of low humidity than most plants.

Comments: During the day, likes high temperatures. Tolerates average temperatures. Feed lightly once or twice a year. Multiply by potting any suckers from around base or by air layering.

SNAKE PLANT
(Sansevieria, hemp plant, or mother-in-law's tongue)
Sansevieria sp.

Foliage: Tall leaves make prime vertical accents in arrangements. The plant also endures where others falter, surviving dim daylight, haphazard watering, heat, dust, and dry air.

Light: Provide bright light, even an east window. Can exist for a long time in dim corners.

Water: Offer low humidity because it is a succulent. Keep soil on the dry side. Water only once every 2 weeks in fall and winter.

Comments: Temperatures in 80s during the day for best growth. Feed no more than once a month and only in spring and summer. Increase by root division or from cuttings of leaf sections. Cuttings of variegated varieties may revert to all green.

SPIDER PLANT
(Airplane plant, ribbon plant, spider ivy)
Chlorophytum comosum

Foliage: Popular and dependable, with long, thin, arching leaves of dark green, often with one or more white stripes down the middle. The stems grow out, produce little white flowers, then plantlets.

Light: Place in bright light, although plant will grow slowly even in a north window. Outdoors, provide shade and wind protection.

Water: Let soil dry, then water and mist generously.

Comments: Maintain temperatures of 60 to 75 degrees. Feed weekly with mild solution to encourage longer leaves and more offspring. Runners will root easily in soil or water before or after separation. Do not feed the runners until they become established. Use standard potting mix.

UMBRELLA PLANT
(Nile grass, umbrella palm, umbrella sedge)
Cyperus alternifolius

Foliage: This plant has feathery top growth that complements the older, coarser foliage. Stiff stems grow from a clump, and palmlike leaves radiate from the top of the stem. Little flowers bloom from June to October and form additional umbrellas above the foliage.

Varieties range from 6 inches to 4 feet tall.

Light: Medium (bright indirect) light except in winter, when high light is better.

Water: Provide constant moisture. Umbrella plant is one of the very few houseplants whose pot can stand in a saucer of water.

Comments: Maintain average temperatures. Feed every 2 weeks during spring and summer. Divide plants or root leaf rosettes.

WANDERING JEW
Tradescantia or Zebrina sp.

Foliage: The two types of wandering Jew are unrelated except in form, but both are no-kill plants with similar red, purple, green, and silver leaf marks, and trailing habit.

Light: Provide full sun to indirect light; the brighter the light, the deeper the colors.

Water: Offer humidity and keep soil evenly moist. Grows in water.

Comments: Maintain average temperatures; avoid cold drafts. Pinch constantly to keep plants from getting leggy, or double the

Wandering Jew

runners back to the soil and pin them down to root. Cuttings root easily at any time.

WEEPING FIG
Ficus benjamina

Foliage: One of the finest indoor trees. Branches weep slightly and have small, shiny leaves.

Light: Medium (bright indirect) light is best; filtered light in summer.

Water: Allow soil to dry between thorough waterings. Mist frequently. Tolerates dry conditions; prefers humidity.

Comments: Average temperatures are fine; avoid cold drafts. Plant gets large; pot up if needed. Feed every 14 days with mild solution. Prune to desired shape in spring. Some leaves yellow and drop off after any move and in winter. Propagate by air layering.

Flowering Plants

ACHIMENES
(Magic flower, monkey-faced pansy, orchid pansy, widow's tears)
Achimenes sp.

Flowers: Showers of colored tubular blooms spring until fall.

Light: Protect from midday sun; likes an east window.

Water: Be sure to keep moist. If it dries, it's instant dormancy.

Comments: For blooming, needs 60-degree night temperatures, up to 80s in daytime. Start rhizomes in moist sphagnum or vermiculite in spring, then transfer several to a pot or hanging basket of half peat and half sand and soil. Feed twice a month during bloom. In late October, decrease water so plants die down naturally. Store unpotted rhizomes in dry sand or vermiculite in 50-degree temperatures until spring. Propagate by stem cuttings in spring, rhizome division when repotting, or seed in winter.

AFRICAN VIOLET
Saintpaulia sp.

Flowers: Flowers come in shades of white and pink to purple, double or single, with rich form variations. Velvety leaves have varied edgings and colors, purple to metallic.

Light: Place in bright indirect (medium) light. East windows are best; north windows in the summer. Plants like artificial light, 14 to 18 hours a day.

Water: Plant in wick-watering pots for best results. Otherwise, water only when soil surface dries. Tepid water in shade will not hurt leaves. Avoid cold water or full sun.

Comments: Maintain high temperatures; keep in warm room, 60 to 75 degrees, day and night. Avoid sudden changes. For humidity, set plants on trays of pebbles; don't mist leaves. Use African violet potting mix, or add peat, perlite, sand, or leaf mold to regular mixes. Feed with an African violet food; dilute some in each watering. Crowns sometimes need dividing. Leaf cuttings usually root easily but rather slowly. Or propagate by seeds or division.

AZALEA
Rhododendron sp.

Flowers: Bright, showy flowers in white or many shades of pink. Will bloom for several weeks indoors.

Light: Give up to 4 hours of direct sunlight daily.

Water: Water generously. After 15 minutes, water again. Or sink whole pots in water for a half hour (never longer).

Comments: Needs cool night temperatures—40 to 65 degrees—to bloom. After bloom, feed with acid fertilizer every 2 weeks until fall, monthly after that. Never feed while in bloom. Summer outdoors in filtered light. Top-dress with acid peat in fall. Water as needed. Propagate by stem cuttings, ground layering, or seed.

BROMELIADS—GENERAL

Flowers: Exotic, stiff leaves and vase-shape trunks with bright, bold, unusual flowers.

Light: Requirements vary. Bright but not full sun for many; others need medium light. The stiffer the leaves, the more light needed.

Water: Keep water in center of cup formed by leaves; water base once a week. Like humidity; don't mist in bright sunlight.

Comments: Plants thrive in commercial soil mix of half fir bark or sphagnum moss, and half sand for good drainage. Roots need little space. Feed little—every 6 to 8 weeks in summer. They form offsets at the base; separate these and pot to multiply stock.

CYCLAMEN
(Poor man's orchid)
Cyclamen persicum

Flowers: Round to heart-shape leaves are mottled and mounded on long, slender stems. It has exquisite blooms with recurved butterfly petals that rise above the foliage in great profusion.

Directory of Houseplants

Light: Give bright light to full sun filtered by curtains. Cyclamen also likes artificial light.

Water: Water from the bottom and never get the leaves wet. The succulent stems grow from a corm slightly concaved at the top, and if the corm holds water, rot sets in.

Comments: Maintain temperatures from 50 to 68 during day; drop 10 degrees at night. This need for low temperatures is the reason cyclamen usually doesn't survive indoors for long periods. Discard without guilt when they go. Start from seeds.

CYMBIDIUM
Cymbidium hybrids

Flowers: Stunning orchids in winter; grassy stems.

Light: Place in high light in winter, medium to high light otherwise. Summer outdoors if possible. Needs 3 weeks with 12 hours of darkness in fall for new bloom.

Water: Keep evenly moist, not soggy. Never allow to dry out.

Comments: Maintain average temperatures; needs 55 degrees or below during the 3 weeks of short days prior to blooming. Use special orchid mix. Fertilize with dilute solution while blooming. Propagate by division, leaving parent plant with 4 stems.

FUCHSIA
(Lady's-eardrops)
Fuchsia sp.

Flowers: The long, pendent blooms have recurved petals about halfway down, then a bell skirt bottom from which the stamens and pistil extend.

Light: Provide bright light, but protect from midday sun. East or west windows are best.

Water: Keep soil evenly moist, not soggy. Plants have shallow roots.

Comments: Keep your house cool at night, 50 to 65 degrees. It will perish in overheated rooms. Feed twice a month when flowering. Reduce both water and food between blooming periods. Pinch to keep bushy. Propagate from stem cuttings.

Upright or trailing, fuchsia produces spectacular bell-like blooms in a wide range of colors.

GARDENIA
(Cape jasmine)
Gardenia jasminoides

Flowers: Shiny-leaved plants with delicate, wildly fragrant flowers, often difficult to grow.

Light: Place in sun in winter, bright shade in summer.

Water: Water heavily. Gardenias can sit with water always in the saucer. Mist plants daily.

Comments: Maintain temperatures in the low 60s to bud, not below 70 once they form. If you buy a plant in bud, remove all but a very few.

Repot every spring in a porous, peat-rich (by half), acid (no lime) soil mix. Feed with special acid food. Put plants outdoors in summer with pots sunk to the rim for constant moisture. Pinch flower buds to encourage winter bloom. Propagate by cuttings or seed.

GLOXINIA
Sinningia sp.

Flowers: Huge, scallop-edge, velvetlike trumpets. They bloom—often white on the outside and edged with brilliant color inside—above a low mound of large leaves.

Light: Offer bright light but not direct sunlight. Too little light creates leggy stems.

Water: Keep soil evenly moist, but avoid waterlogging. Keep water off the hairy foliage and the top of the tuber by watering around the edge of the pot or from the bottom.

Comments: Likes high temperaures and humidity except during dormancy. Use African violet soil mix. At dormancy, store in dark place at 50 degrees; repot when growth begins. Feed lightly every few weeks beginning as soon as flower buds develop. Start new plants from seed, or root leaf cuttings at the base, bracing leaves with sticks.

HIBISCUS
(Chinese hibiscus, Chinese rose)
Hibiscus sp.

Flowers: The showy blooms come in bright shades of red, pink, purple, orange, yellow, and white, and are 4 to 8 inches across. Each one lasts only a day and stays lovely even without water.

Light: Provide full sun for bloom. Even without flowers, hibiscus is an attractive foliage plant.

Water: Keep soil evenly moist when plant is in flower, on the dry side at other times. Likes humidity.

Comments: Keep plants in a warm spot when growing and blooming, a cool place at other times. In March, before new growth starts, prune plants back by half and repot if necessary. Use a standard potting soil and feed lightly only when in growth or bloom. Pinch tips to keep plants compact and bushy. Summer plants outdoors for maximum

bloom in the summer and fall. Propagate by seed or tip cuttings from new growth.

KALANCHOE
(Aurora borealis plant, Christmas kalanchoe)
Kalanchoe blossfeldiana

Flowers: In full sunlight, kalanchoe's leaf edges are reddish, and bright clusters of tiny flowers bloom for long periods. Flowers form only when days are short, so the plant will not bloom if it gets any night light at all.

Light: Give full sun in spring, fall, and winter. Avoid direct sun during the hottest part of day in summer.

Water: Let soil dry between waterings. Water more frequently until the flowers fade, then keep soil on the dry side for a month or two with just enough moisture to keep the leaves from shriveling.

Comments: Place where nights are cool, down to 50 degrees. Prune well back after flowers fade, then put in shade outside. Bring back to a sunny window in September, or take stem or leaf cuttings for new plants.

LADY'S-SLIPPER
(Slipper orchid)
Paphiopedilum sp.

Flowers: Tricky to grow, produces pouchlike blooms once a year.

Light: High light in winter; medium (bright indirect) the rest of the year. Eastern exposure is best.

Water: Keep growing medium constantly moist and humidity high. Don't let plant become dry.

Comments: Maintain average temperatures. Drop by 10 degrees at night. Use orchid potting mix and shallow pot; repot yearly to change medium. Feed every 14 days in spring and summer; monthly in fall and winter. Propagate by division or seed.

POINSETTIA
Euphorbia pulcherrima

Flowers: Bright red, pink, or white colors in large showy blooms.

Light: Provide bright light until plant reaches peak of bloom, when it can survive with less. Avoid drafts. Most important: enjoy the plant. Place it accordingly.

Water: Be sure both the pot and any foil or paper wrapping allow drainage. Water enough to drain through, then check plant daily and water again when the surface begins to dry.

Comments: Place plants in a cool room, especially at night. Feed within 10 days after purchase. Feed monthly after that. Poinsettias root from stem cuttings and grow easily, but they will not form buds unless they have 12 to 14 hours of complete darkness each day.

SPATHIPHYLLUM
(White anthurium, peace lily, spathe flower)
Spathiphyllum sp.

Flowers: Foliage looks much like smaller aspidistra; sword-shape leaves grow 1½ feet long. The pale green sheath turns white as it opens. The true flowers are tiny and surround a slender protruding stalk. Each bloom lasts for weeks, usually in January and February.

Light: Provide bright light in winter, diffused light in summer. Plants will bloom in shade, but with sparse, undersize flowers.

Water: Keep soil evenly moist. Increase humidity.

Comments: Place in a warm room. Feed every 2 months from March to September. Divide the roots of pot-bound plants after flowering. Pot up each spring. When leaf tips yellow, check for too much or not enough water, or insufficient food.

SUCCULENTS— GENERAL

Flowers: The unique forms and sculpted shapes result partly from stored water.

Light: Place most succulents in south windows. Some need protection from intense afternoon sun. When you move them outdoors for the summer, ease them into sun or open shade gradually; otherwise, they will cook in their own juices and turn transparent.

Water: During fall and winter, water only enough to keep the roots and soil from drying, not enough to encourage new growth. The plants will take considerably more water during their active growing and blooming time, in spring and summer. Be sure their pots provide drainage; water every other week.

Comments: Leaves fall off at the slightest pressure. Pot with a layer of drainage in the bottom, preferably gravel, broken pottery, or similar jagged-edge material. Buy potting mix for cactus and succulents. Leave an inch at the top of the pot. Feed succulents frequently but lightly. Succulents multiply easily from cuttings, seeds, grafts, or offsets.

TUBEROUS BEGONIA
Begonia x tuberhybrida

Flowers: Spectacular blooms in many sizes, shapes, and colors.

Light: Expose to medium light during active growth, dark during dormancy.

Water: Keep constantly moist during active growth. Water less after foliage starts to yellow. Stop during dormancy. Raise humidity.

Tuberous Begonia

WAX PLANT
(Hoya, hindu-rope, honey plant)
Hoya sp.

Flowers: A dozen varieties, all attractive as foliage plants with thick, succulent, waxlike leaves of varied markings. The clusters of star-shape, fragrant flowers are creamy velvet with a perfect dark pink star in the center, blue-white with red centers, or yellow-green.

Light: Give bright light, up to 4 hours of sun a day. Lives for years, unblooming, in shade.

Water: Water generously during bloom. Keep almost dry otherwise.

Comments: Plant tubers, hollow side up and barely exposed, in shallow pots; use soil high in organic matter. Keep moist and at 70 degrees to spur growth. Water and feed regularly. Water less after blooms fade; store clean, dry in cool, dry, dark place. Propagate by cutting shoots off tubers. Use as tip cuttings.

Comments: Average temperatures when active, low 60s in dormancy. Feed every second month. Use extra-rich soil with sand and leaf mold. Tie plants to supports for best growth. Keep plants pot-bound for many flowers. Never remove a stub where the flowers appear or you will be cutting off the next blooms. Propagate with tip cuttings.

First Aid for Plants

Symptom: Leaf tips turn brown; lower leaves turn yellow and drop off. Stems get soft and mushy, then turn brown. Soil is soggy, and slimy scum forms on edges of pots.

Cause & Cure: Too much water. Allow soil to dry completely before watering again. Repot if soil is soggy. Make sure plant has adequate drainage. Don't let it sit in water in saucer. Water less often.

Symptom: Leaf tips turn yellow, then turn brown and dry up. Bottom leaves turn yellow.

Cause & Cure: Too little water. Water plant thoroughly by immersing the whole pot in water. Let excess drain away. Water on a strict schedule.

Symptom: Leaves look faded or have yellow or brown "burned" spots. Foliage plants turn brown.

Cause & Cure: Too much light. Move plant out of bright light. Ease up on artificial light.

Symptom: Plant develops long, spindly stems. New growth is weak and pale; leaves are undersize.

Cause & Cure: Too little light. Move plant to a location that gets more light, or supplement natural light with artificial light.

Symptom: Plant grows quickly, but new growth is weak and spindly or streaked with yellow. A crusty scum may form on pots.

Cause & Cure: Too much fertilizer. Flush fertilizer buildup out of the soil and off pot rims by watering the plant several times an hour with tepid water. Let excess moisture run out the bottom. Stop fertilizing for a while, and reduce dosage or frequency.

Symptom: Leaves look yellow but veins are green. New growth is weak and droopy.

Cause & Cure: Too little fertilizer. Set up a fertilizing schedule based on plant's needs and the season.

Symptom: Edges of leaves curl under and turn crispy and brown.

Cause & Cure: Too little humidity or temperature is too high—or both. Add humidity to the air by misting plants or installing a home humidifier. Move to a cooler spot.

Houseplant Pests

Mealybugs These white cottony blobs are apt to be your worst headache. They're sometimes hard to eradicate because they're protected by a water-resistant wax. Dab each bug with a cotton swab dipped in rubbing alcohol, and rinse leaves with clear, cool water. Or use a houseplant miticide, and rinse plants when mealybugs are eradicated.

If you have African violet, fuchsia, coleus, and wax vine, be on the alert. Regular cleanings help prevent outbreak.

Red Spider Mites These tiny bugs feed on the undersides of leaves, spinning fine webs along veins and leaves. They give a plant a rusty look in the early stages, and a gray webby look with anemic foliage later on. Look for them on azalea, hydrangea, and ivy.

If possible, take plant outside and flush bottoms of leaves with a light spray from a garden hose. Or mix a mild soap (not detergent) into a pan of lukewarm water, producing a lather. Cover the top of the pot with foil to hold the dirt, upend the plant, and swish the foliage through the suds. Rinse well with clear water. Follow this procedure once a week until pests are gone. If you use a miticide, wash the leaves to remove the webs.

Scale Scale looks like little green or brown ovals. Scales line up along the main veins of the plant and cause it to lose color, yellow, and die. Prime targets are ferns, palms, and rubber plants.

Gently scrape the scale off with a soft toothbrush or your fingernail. Wash the plant with lukewarm, soapy water.

Aphids These greenish white or black insects cluster in the open where they're easily detected.

Use the tepid, soapy water wash and clear rinse recommended for red spider mites. Or spray with a miticide and rinse when pests have been eradicated.

At least once a year give your houseplants and their pots a thorough housecleaning. Throw out sickly plants before their ailments spread to healthy ones.

Index